Editor
Eric Migliaccio

Managing Editor
Ina Massler Levin, M.A.

Illustrator
Denise Bauer

Art Manager
Kevin Barnes

Art Director
CJae Froshay

Imaging
Rosa C. See

Publisher
Mary D. Smith, M.S. Ed.

Grades 4 & Up

Fun with Homonyms

Crossword Puzzles and Word Searches

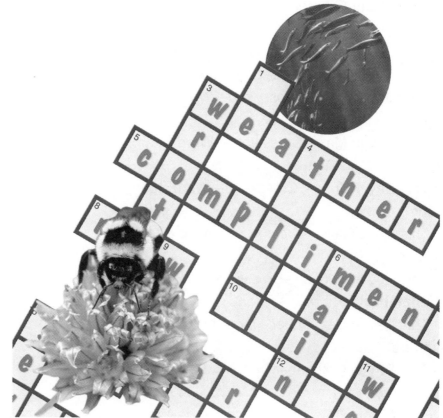

Author

Judy Wilson Goddard

Teacher Created Resources, Inc.
6421 Industry Way
Westminster, CA 92683
www.teachercreated.com
ISBN-1-4206-3143-8

©2005 Teacher Created Resources, Inc.

Made in U.S.A.

S0-AUT-836

Table of Contents

Introduction 2

January 3
This Day in January—Crossword—Word Search

February 6
This Day in February—Crossword—Word Search

March 9
This Day in March—Crossword—Word Search

April 12
This Day in April—Crossword—Word Search

May 15
This Day in May—Crossword—Word Search

June 18
This Day in June—Crossword—Word Search

July 21
This Day in July—Crossword—Word Search

August 24
This Day in August—Crossword—Word Search

September 27
This Day in September—Crossword—Word Search

October 30
This Day in October—Crossword—Word Search

November 33
This Day in November—Crossword—Word Search

December 36
This Day in December—Crossword—Word Search

Holidays 39
Holidays of the Year—Crossword—Word Search

Answer Key 42

Introduction

This book's goal is to incorporate homonyms with cultural literacy information that is presented in calendar order, several for each month of the year. In this way, a lesson in language arts is combined with a lesson in cultural literacy. Students will interpret vocabulary in context, and practice reading and understanding passages, while focusing on homonyms and cultural literacy. This book features cultural literacy sentences for certain days and holidays of the year. Each sentence includes spaces that need to be filled in with homonyms. Students are instructed to circle the correct homonym.

In addition, a word search and crossword puzzle are provided for each month and for a special holiday section at the end. Not only are these exercises fun for the students, but they give them more practice with homonyms.

This Day in January

Directions: Circle the correct homonyms to complete each sentence. Remember that homonyms are words that sound alike but have a different meaning and a different spelling.

January 1

Happy (**Knew, New**) Year! It is a time to (**pause, paws**), look back on the past, and look forward to the future as we (**ring, wring**) in the (**new, knew**) year.

January 5

Nellie T. Ross became the first woman governor of the United States on January 5, 1925. She became governor of Wyoming after her husband (**died, dyed**) while in office and she was nominated (**to, too, two**) fill the remainder of his term.

January 8

The King is born! Rock 'n' (**role, roll**) performer Elvis Presley was born on January 8, 1935. He had many hit singles, including "(**Blew, Blue**) Suede Shoes" and "Love Me Tender."

January 17

Benjamin Franklin was born on this date in 1706. He was a leader, printer, scientist, and writer. As a scientist, he conducted many experiments. On a stormy day when the (**weather, whether**) was (**ruff, rough**), he (**flew, flu**) his kite into lightning. When the key on his kite and the lightning collided, he was able to prove that lightning contained electricity.

January 22

The first postal route was established on January 22, 1672. Through (**rein, rain, reign**), snow, sleet, and (**hale, hail**), the (**mail, male**) was delivered between Boston, Massachusetts, and New York, New York.

January 25

On January 25, 1961, the 37th U.S. president, John F. Kennedy, held the first televised presidential news conference. Millions of Americans saw and (**heard, herd**) the broadcast. This began a new era in communication.

January 31

Jackie Robinson was (**born, borne**) on January 31, 1919. He is known for integrating the game of baseball. He became the first African-American major league baseball player. It was a (**grate, great**) day for (**him, hymn**) and all future African-American players.

January Crossword

Find the homonyms for . . .

Across
2. bowed
3. wear/ware
5. miner
6. whether
7. peal
8. complement
10. wail
12. foul
14. in
15. ruff
16. chord

Down
1. ball
2. bettor
4. bode
5. mourning
8. sealing
9. mall
11. hale
12. fined
13. sore

January Word Search

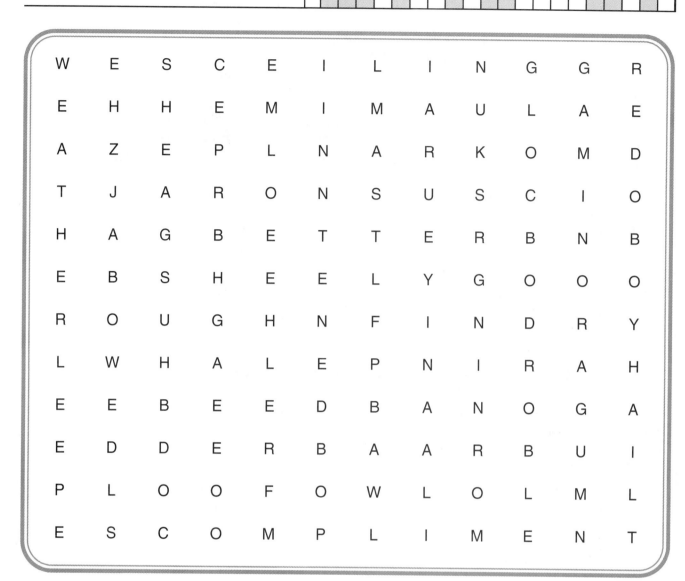

```
W  E  S  C  E  I  L  I  N  G  G  R
E  H  H  E  M  I  M  A  U  L  A  E
A  Z  E  P  L  N  A  R  K  O  M  D
T  J  A  R  O  N  S  U  S  C  I  O
H  A  G  B  E  T  T  E  R  B  N  B
E  B  S  H  E  E  L  Y  G  O  O  O
R  O  U  G  H  N  F  I  N  D  R  Y
L  W  H  A  L  E  P  N  I  R  A  H
E  E  B  E  E  D  B  A  N  O  G  A
E  D  D  E  R  B  A  A  R  B  U  I
P  L  O  O  F  O  W  L  O  L  M  L
E  S  C  O  M  P  L  I  M  E  N  T
```

In the puzzle above, find the homonyms for . . .

were/wear	fined	in
complement	mall	peal
whether	ball	wail
sealing	miner	hale
mourning	ruff	bowed
bettor	chord	bode
sore	foul	

This Day in February

Directions: Circle the correct homonyms to complete each sentence. Remember that ĪĬ are words that sound alike but have a different meaning and a different spelling.

February 2

Let's celebrate! Today is Groundhog Day. If the groundhog wakes up from his long winter snooze, pokes his head out of his hole, and sees his shadow, we will (**halve, have**) six more weeks of winter. If he does (**knot, not**) (**see, sea**) his shadow, summer is on the way.

February 7

Laura Ingles Wilder was born on this date in 1867. She (**wrote, rote**) *Little House on the Prairie* and other books that tell about pioneer life in the Midwest. Her works received much (**prays, praise, preys**); later, a television series was based on her work.

February 11

Thomas Edison was born on this date in 1847. He said, "Genius is 1 percent inspiration and 99 percent perspiration." He had 1,093 patents in his lifetime. For (**instants, instance**), he invented the electric light bulb.

February 19

Nicholas Copernicus was born on this date in 1473. He was an astronomer—one who studies the stars, planets, and galaxies. He developed the idea that (**hour, our**) earth moves around the (**sun, son**). Before this time, astronomers thought the earth stood still and other heavenly bodies moved around it.

February 23

Johann Gutenberg was born on February 23, 1395. He invented a way to print from movable type. Before his invention, (**all, awl**) books were written (**buy, by, bye**) hand.

February 26

Levi Strauss was born on this date (**in, inn**) 1829. He created the first blue jeans. Do you (**ware, wear**) Levi's?

February 29

Every ten years, we have 29 days in February. We add this extra day to make our calendar year more nearly match the movement of the earth around the (**son, sun**), (**which, witch**) takes 365.25 days. When we add an extra day, (**it's, its**) called a leap year. All other years are called common years.

February Crossword

Find the homonyms for . . .

Across

2. son
4. deer
6. plain
7. blue
10. won
11. peace
13. feat
14. aloud
15. hear

Down

1. grate
2. suite
3. knot
5. maid
6. prays/preys
7. beet
8. hole
9. meat
12. roll
13. four/fore
15. hymn

February Word Search

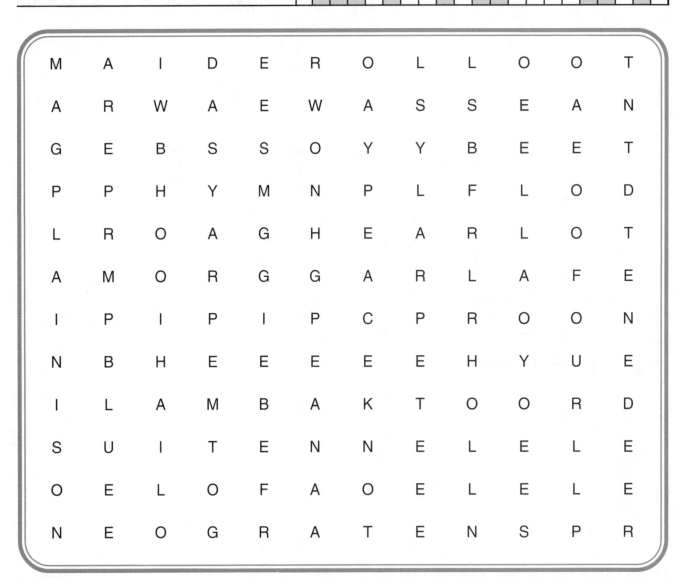

M	A	I	D	E	R	O	L	L	O	O	T
A	R	W	A	E	W	A	S	S	E	A	N
G	E	B	S	S	O	Y	Y	B	E	E	T
P	P	H	Y	M	N	P	L	F	L	O	D
L	R	O	A	G	H	E	A	R	L	O	T
A	M	O	R	G	G	A	R	L	A	F	E
I	P	I	P	I	P	C	P	R	O	O	N
N	B	H	E	E	E	E	E	H	Y	U	E
I	L	A	M	B	A	K	T	O	O	R	D
S	U	I	T	E	N	N	E	L	E	L	E
O	E	L	O	F	A	O	E	L	E	L	E
N	E	O	G	R	A	T	E	N	S	P	R

In the puzzle above, find the homonyms for . .

dear	feet	praise/preys
sun	him	blew
allowed	meet	great
here	plane	one
made	beat	role
piece	for/fore	whole
sweet	not	

This Day in March

Directions: Circle the correct homonyms to complete each sentence. Remember that homonyms are words that sound alike but have a different meaning and a different spelling.

March 2

Theodore Seuss Geisel was born on this date in 1904. His pen name was Dr. Seuss. He wrote such books as *Green Eggs and Ham* and *The Cat In The Hat.* Caution: (**you'll, yule**) fall out of (**yore, your**) seat from laughing so much at these characters. In 1984, Dr. Seuss received the Pulitzer Prize—an annual award for outstanding work in journalism, literature, and music.

March 7

Victor Farris was born on this date in 1985. He owned 200 other patents, among them one for the paper milk carton. A patent gives legal ownership so that only the owner of the patent can make, use, and (**cell, sell**) an invention or grant others that (**right, write**).

March 19

Don't forget to set your clocks (**forward, foreword**)! Daylight Savings Time (DST) was (**past, passed**) on this date in 1928. It lasts from the first Sunday in April until the last Sunday in October. By setting our clocks forward one (**hour, our**), we get extra daylight and are able to conserve electricity.

March 21

Yay! Today is the start of spring. (**It's, Its**) also called the Vernal Equinox. "Vernal" means "of or relating to spring" and "equinox" means a time when the (**son, sun**) crosses the equator and day and (**night, knight**) are of equal length.

March 23

"Give me liberty (**oar, ore, or**) give me death," stated Patrick Henry on March 23, 1775. This American patriot believed in freedom and (**piece, peace**), even if it meant war and possibly death. He did not die in (**vain, vein**); he is remembered as a national hero.

March 28

Nathaniel Briggs received a patent (**for, four, fore**) the first washing machine on this date (**inn, in**) 1879.

March 31

The Eiffel Tower in Paris, France, was completed on March 31, 1889. (**Halve, Have**) you ever (**bin, been**) to Paris? (**Would, Wood**) you like to go?

March Crossword

Find the homonyms for . . .

Across

2. ate
5. chili
6. piece
7. plumb
11. forth
13. vein/vane
15. write
16. maid
17. effect

Down

1. bin
3. tow
4. wood
5. sense/scents
6. pour/pore
7. principle
8. knight
9. borne
10. their/they're
12. patients
14. sail

March Word Search

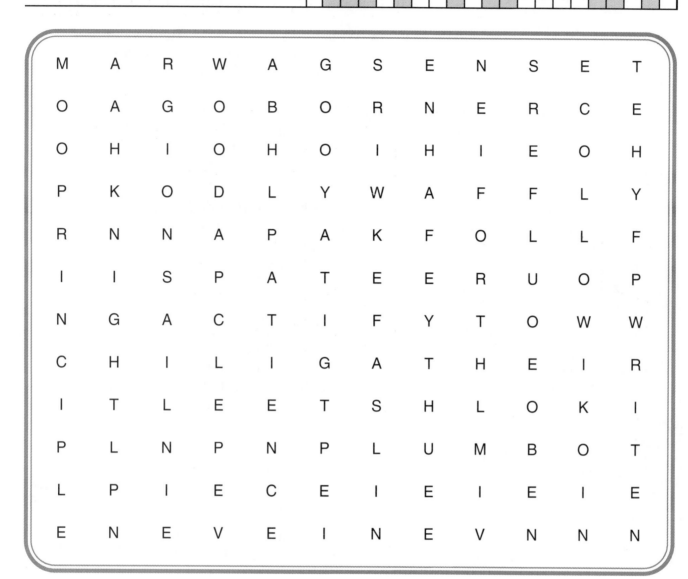

```
M  A  R  W  A  G  S  E  N  S  E  T
O  A  G  O  B  O  R  N  E  R  C  E
O  H  I  O  H  O  I  H  E  E  O  H
P  K  O  D  L  Y  W  A  F  F  L  Y
R  N  N  A  P  A  K  F  O  L  L  F
I  I  S  P  A  T  E  E  R  U  O  P
N  G  A  C  T  I  F  Y  T  O  W  W
C  H  I  L  I  G  A  T  H  E  I  R
I  T  L  E  E  T  S  H  L  O  K  I
P  L  N  P  N  P  L  U  M  B  O  T
L  P  I  E  C  E  I  E  I  E  I  E
E  N  E  V  E  I  N  E  V  N  N  N
```

In the puzzle above, find the homonyms for . . .

affect	chilly	peace
fourth	sale	would
principal	been	born
there/they're	patients	plum
cents/scents	vain/vane	night
right	eight	poor/pore
toe	made	

This Day in April

Directions: Circle the correct homonyms to complete each sentence. Remember that homonyms are words that sound alike but have a different meaning and a different spelling.

April 2

Hans Christian Anderson was born on April 2, 1860. He wrote over 160 (**ferry, fairy**) (**tales, tails**). Two of his famous stories were *The Ugly Duckling* and *The Princess and the Pea.*

April 5

Joseph Lister, M.D., was born on April 5, 1827. He discovered modern antiseptic surgery, which had a great (**affect, effect**) on medicine. An antiseptic cleans and kills germs; this discovery greatly reduced the number of deaths. Before Dr. Lister's discovery, the death rate of surgery (**patience, patients**) was (**very, vary**) high.

April 6

The first modern Olympic games were held in Athens, Greece, on this date in 1896. The Olympics are the oldest and most famous international sporting contest. Both the Winter Olympic Games and the Summer Olympic Games are held in a different city every (**forth, fourth**) year, when athletes from (**awl, all**) around the world compete.

April 14

The S.S. Titanic sank on this date in 1912, after hitting an iceberg in the North Atlantic Ocean. Unfortunately, 1,517 passengers (**dyed, died**) at (**sea, see**).

April 15

On April 15, 1955, McDonald's started serving hamburgers at a restaurant (**in, inn**) Des Plaines, Illinois. Ten years later, (**their, they're, there**) were 4,600 restaurants in 23 different countries.

April 18

Paul Revere's Ride took place on this date in 1775. He (**road, rode**) on horseback, from Boston (**to, too, two**) Lexington. The purpose of his journey was (**to, too, two**) warn the American soldiers that the British soldiers were coming.

April 26

Charles Richter was born on this date in 1900. Thirty-five years later, he developed the Richter Scale, (**witch, which**) measures the magnitude of earthquakes. Magnitude refers to the strength, not the (**sighs, size**), of the earthquake.

April 29

Gideon Sundback patented the zipper on April 29, 1917. A patent gives legal ownership for 17 years. During that (**time, thyme**) only the owner of the patent can make, use, and (**sell, cell**) the invention.

April Crossword

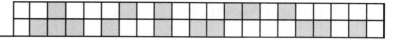

Find the homonyms for . . .

Across	Down
2. cell	1. no
3. one	2. sighs
4. waive	5. vary
8. road	6. reed
9. ferry	7. sites/sights
12. dyed	10. lead
14. tails	11. wear/where
15. forth	13. affect
16. seemed	14. through
18. tacks	17. male

April Word Search

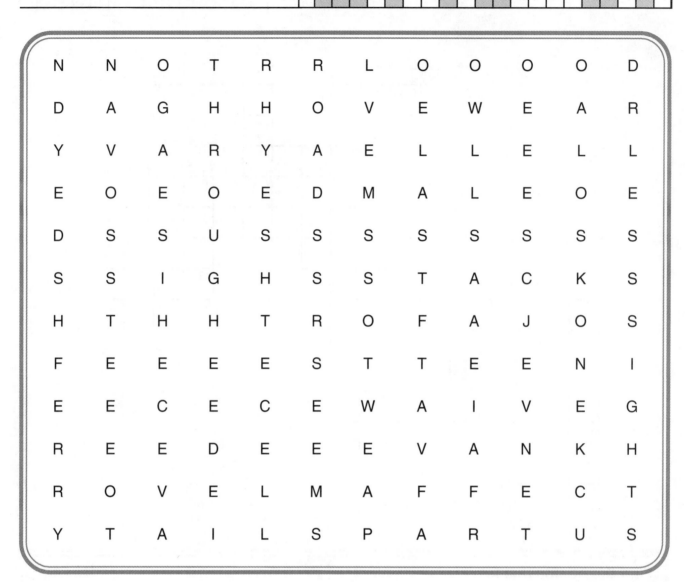

```
N  N  O  T  R  R  R  L  O  O  O  O  D
D  A  G  H  H  O  V  E  W  E  A  R
Y  V  A  R  Y  A  E  L  L  E  L  L
E  O  E  O  E  D  M  A  L  E  O  E
D  S  S  U  S  S  S  S  S  S  S  S
S  S  I  G  H  S  S  T  A  C  K  S
H  T  H  H  T  R  O  F  A  J  O  S
F  E  E  E  E  S  T  T  E  E  N  I
E  E  C  E  C  E  W  A  I  V  E  G
R  E  E  D  E  E  E  V  A  N  K  H
R  O  V  E  L  M  A  F  F  E  C  T
Y  T  A  I  L  S  P  A  R  T  U  S
```

In the puzzle above, find the homonyms for . . .

tales	mail	died
fairy	sell	wave
know	very	effect
led	cites/sites	won
seams	read	rode
threw	size	tax
fourth	ware	

This Day in May

Directions: Circle the correct homonyms to complete each sentence. Remember that homonyms are words that sound alike but have a different meaning and a different spelling.

May 2

Leonardo de Vinci died on this date in 1519. He was a scientist, sculptor, painter, and architect; and he also designed bridges, highways, weapons, costumes, and scientific instruments. He was an expert in (**all, awl**) of these fields; however, he is most remembered (**for, four, fore**) his (**canvas, canvass**) painting of Mona Lisa.

May 6

George Herman Ruth, nicknamed "Babe," hit his first home run on this date in 1915. He continued hitting homers and set a record in 1935 with 714. This record stood (**fore, four, for**) 39 years! It wasn't until 1974 that Hank Aaron was able to (**break, brake**) the record.

May 10

On May 10, 1872, Victoria Woodhull became the first woman (**too, two, to**) run for the office of president of the United States.

May 14

Gabriel Fahrenheit was born on this date in 1686. He created the Fahrenheit temperature scale. In 1714, he created the mercury thermometer that is still (**in, inn**) use today. His scale marks 32 degrees as the freezing point of water and 212 degrees as the boiling point. Everyone (**aught, ought**) to (**know, no**) this!

May 17

The U.S. Supreme Court (**maid, made**) an important decision on May 17, 1954, in the case of Brown vs. Board of Education of Topeka, Kansas. The United States Supreme Court determined that segregation (**in, inn**) public schools was unconstitutional.

May 24

Samuel Morse sent the first telegraph message on this date in 1844. This invention was the first (**mowed, mode**) of communication between (**too, to, two**) distant places.

May 28

Jim Thorpe was born on May 28, 1886. He was (**won, one**) of the world's most versatile athletes. He played professional football, major-league baseball, and gained fame as a track-and-field champion. This athlete had lots of (**mussel, muscle**).

May Crossword

Find the homonyms for . . .

Across

2. guessed
4. rode
8. peddle
9. loan
10. there/they're
11. one
14. reed
15. mussel
16. to/two
17. won

Down

1. vain/vein
3. sees/seas
5. canvas
6. fore/four
7. borne
8. peek/pique
10. their/they're
12. or/ore
13. rein/reign
15. mowed

May Word Search

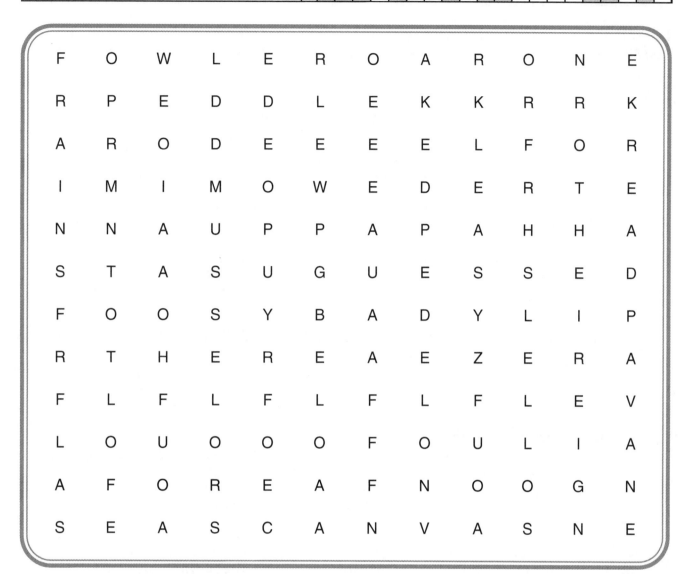

```
F  O  W  L  E  R  O  A  R  O  N  E
R  P  E  D  D  L  E  K  K  R  R  K
A  R  O  D  E  E  E  E  L  F  O  R
I  M  I  M  O  W  E  D  E  R  T  E
N  N  A  U  P  P  A  P  A  H  H  A
S  T  A  S  U  G  U  E  S  S  E  D
F  O  O  S  Y  B  A  D  Y  L  I  P
R  T  H  E  R  E  A  E  Z  E  R  A
F  L  F  L  F  L  F  L  F  L  E  V
L  O  U  O  O  O  F  O  U  L  I  A
A  F  O  R  E  A  F  N  O  O  G  N
S  E  A  S  C  A  N  V  A  S  N  E
```

In the puzzle above, find the homonyms for . . .

seize/sees	pedal	or, ore
won	there	red
mode	fowl	for, four
muscle	foul	lone
peak	rain, rein	road
their	reins, reigns	vain, vein
guest	canvass	

This Day in June

Directions: Circle the correct homonyms to complete each sentence. Remember that homonyms are words that sound alike but have a different meaning and a different spelling.

June 2

On June 2, 1941, baseball (**great, grate**) Lou Gehrig (**died, dyed**) at the age of 37. He lost his battle to a disease that bears his name; (**its, it's**) called Lou Gehrig's disease.

June 6

Today is D-Day. On June 6, 1944, during World War II, the Allies (British, Canadians, and Americans) invaded the beaches of Normandy, France. This famous (**beech, beach**) invasion (**lead, led**) to France's freedom from Germany.

June 8

Ice cream was first advertised and sold (**in, inn**) the United States on this date in 1786. At last, apple (**pi, pie**) could (**be, bee**) served ala mode!

June 13

"You (**halve, have**) the (**right, write**) to remain silent…" On June 13, 1966, it became law that when someone is arrested, he (**oar, or**) she doesn't have to say anything until a lawyer is present. These are called the Miranda Rights.

June 16

Counting 5, 4, 3, 2, 1, and blastoff! Russian Valentine Tereshkova became the first woman in space on June 16, 1963. The Russians clearly (**beet, beat**) the United States on this (**one, won**); it was twenty years before an American woman (**made, maid**) the trip. Sally Ride became the first American woman in space in 1983.

June 21

Today is the traditional day marking the beginning of summer. It's also called Summer Solstice, because the sun is farthest from the equator and the (**raze, rays**) from the sun warm us. It is the longest day of the year, because (**there, their, they're**) are the most daylight (**ours, hours**).

June 27

Today is the birthday of Helen Keller. She was born on this date in 1880. She was blind and deaf. Even though she could not (**here, hear**) or (**see, sea**), she learned to communicate through Braille and sign language. She even learned to (**read, reed**). Her teacher was Anne Sullivan.

June Crossword

Find the homonyms for . . .

Across

4. dyed
5. beat
6. ours
9. grown
10. raze
11. hi
12. cell
14. great
17. wave

Down

1. lead
2. bear
3. ware
5. beech
6. have
7. prose
8. four/for
12. so
13. led
15. read
16. teem

June Word Search

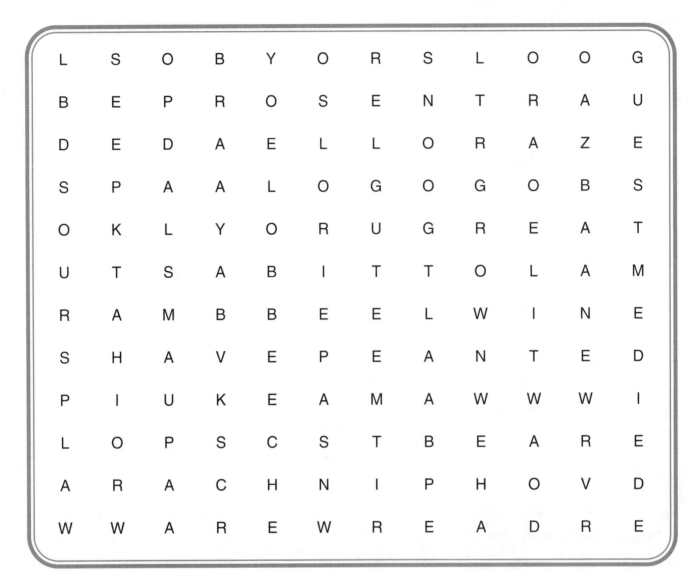

L	S	O	B	Y	O	R	S	L	O	O	G
B	E	P	R	O	S	E	N	T	R	A	U
D	E	D	A	E	L	L	O	R	A	Z	E
S	P	A	A	L	O	G	O	G	O	B	S
O	K	L	Y	O	R	U	G	R	E	A	T
U	T	S	A	B	I	T	T	O	L	A	M
R	A	M	B	B	E	E	L	W	I	N	E
S	H	A	V	E	P	E	A	N	T	E	D
P	I	U	K	E	A	M	A	W	W	W	I
L	O	P	S	C	S	T	B	E	A	R	E
A	R	A	C	H	N	I	P	H	O	V	D
W	W	A	R	E	W	R	E	A	D	R	E

In the puzzle above, find the homonyms for . . .

guessed	beach	whine
waive	halve	pros
bare	led	hours
grate	cell	rays
groan	beet	team
lead	sew	reed
wear	dyed	

This Day in July

Directions: Circle the correct homonyms to complete each sentence. Remember that homonyms are words that sound alike but have a different meaning and a different spelling.

July 5

Tennis anyone? Arthur Ashe became the first African-American to win the men's tennis singles championship at Wimbledon. It was a (**grate, great**) day for (**hymn, him**) and it turned the (**tied, tide**) for other African-Americans in the field of tennis.

July 10

On this date in 1790, Washington, D.C., was chosen as the (**cite, sight, site**) of the (**capital, capitol**) of the United States of America.

July 13

Women began competing in the Olympics on this date in 1908. (**Yule, You'll**) be surprised to (**no, know**) that it was just twelve years after the first Olympics began in 1896.

July 15

"Twas the night before Christmas…" Clement Moore wrote the Christmas poem, "A Visit from St. Nicholas." He was born on July 15, 1779. "And to (**all, awl**) a good (**knight, night**)."

July 16

Burr! Roald Amundsen discovered the South (**Pole, Poll**). He was born on this date (**inn, in**) 1872.

July 20

Counting 5, 4, 3, 2, 1, and blastoff! On July 20, 1969, Neil Armstrong stepped off Apollo 11 and became the first person (**too, to**) set his (**feet, feat**) on the moon. After he took the first step, he stated, "That's (**one, won**) small step for man and (**one, won**) giant leap for mankind." This happened just (**ate, eight**) years after Alan Shepard became the first American in space on May 5, 1961.

July 24

Amelia Earhart was born on this date in 1897. She (**maid, made**) the first solo flight (**buy, by**) a woman. The flight was across the Atlantic Ocean from Canada to Ireland.

July Crossword

Find the homonyms for . . .

Across

4. mail
5. hour
8. knew
10. night
11. him
13. aloud
16. pail
18. tied

Down

1. no
2. capital
3. sell
6. wring
7. son
8. knot
9. died
12. poll
14. ate
15. sight/cite
17. awl

July Word Search

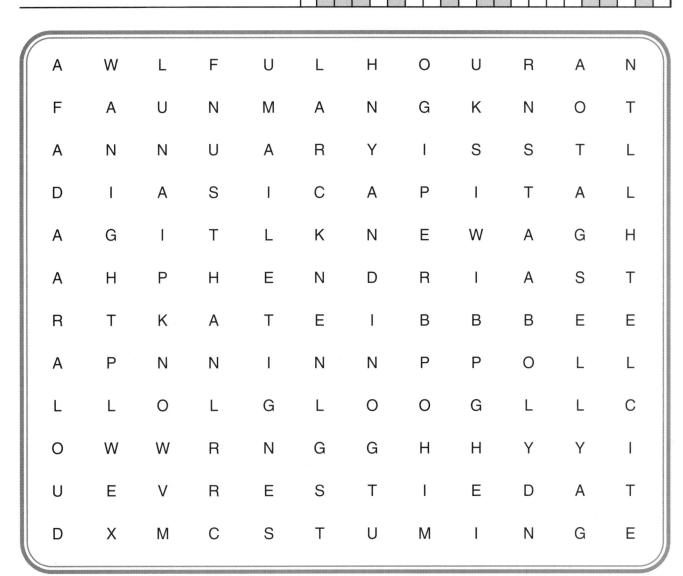

```
A  W  L  F  U  L  H  O  U  R  A  N
F  A  U  N  M  A  N  G  K  N  O  T
A  N  N  U  A  R  Y  I  S  S  T  L
D  I  A  S  I  C  A  P  I  T  A  L
A  G  I  T  L  K  N  E  W  A  G  H
A  H  P  H  E  N  D  R  I  A  S  T
R  T  K  A  T  E  I  B  B  B  E  E
A  P  N  N  I  N  N  P  P  O  L  L
L  L  O  L  G  L  O  O  G  L  L  C
O  W  W  R  N  G  G  H  H  Y  Y  I
U  E  V  R  E  S  T  I  E  D  A  T
D  X  M  C  S  T  U  M  I  N  G  E
```

In the puzzle above, find the homonyms for . . .

all	male	hymn
do/due	pale	not
no	pole	ring
our	sun	capitol
site/sight	new	cell
allowed	tide	fawn
eight	knight	

This Day in August

Directions: Circle the correct homonyms to complete each sentence. Remember that homonyms are words that sound alike but have a different meaning and a different spelling.

August 3

Columbus sailed westward from Spain on this date in 1492. Three ships—the *Nina,* the *Pinta,* and the *Santa Maria*—(**maid, made**) the voyage. We celebrate his discovery of America on the second Monday of October. (**Its, It's**) a national holiday.

August 4

Federal income (**tacks, tax**) was first collected in the United States on August 4, 1862. This (**tacks, tax**) is the major source of government income.

August 8

An artificial (**hart, heart**) pump was successfully implanted (**for, fore, four**) the first time on August 8, 1966.

August 12

The first American police force was established on August 12, 1658. American policemen are known as "cops" or "coppers." (**Sum, Some**) people believe the name comes from the eight-pointed copper star once worn (**bye, by**) policemen.

August 22

Clara Barton, a Civil (**War, Wore**) nurse, founded the first local chapter of the American Red Cross on this date in 1881. The Red Cross is now an international agency that helps the victims of war (**oar, ore, or**) disaster.

August 24

The British Army burned the president's home on this date in 1814. It was rebuilt and painted white; and thereafter, it was called the White House. The White House continues to be the (**residence, residents**) of the president of the United States.

August 30

Guion Bluford, Jr., became the first African-American astronaut to travel in space on this date in 1983. He made a six-day voyage in the space shuttle Challenger. Six days in space—that's a long time, almost a (**whole, hole**) (**weak, week**).

August Crossword

©Teacher Created Resources, Inc.

#3143 Fun with Homonyms

Find the homonyms for . . .

Across
1. forth
4. pain
6. pare/pair
7. hair
9. lynx
11. carat
12. root
14. stares
16. pale
18. plain
19. some

Down
1. fairy
2. residents
3. whole
5. weak
8. writes
10. fair
13. tale
15. steal
17. allowed

August Word Search

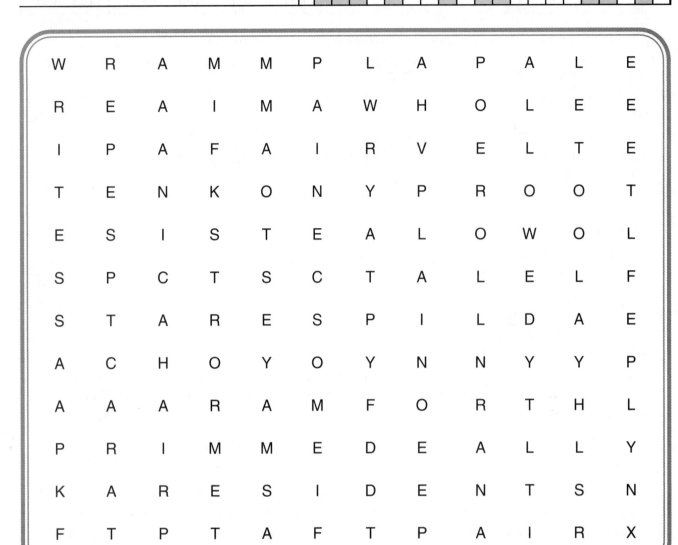

W	R	A	M	M	P	L	A	P	A	L	E
R	E	A	I	M	A	W	H	O	L	E	E
I	P	A	F	A	I	R	V	E	L	T	E
T	E	N	K	O	N	Y	P	R	O	O	T
E	S	I	S	T	E	A	L	O	W	O	L
S	P	C	T	S	C	T	A	L	E	L	F
S	T	A	R	E	S	P	I	L	D	A	E
A	C	H	O	Y	O	Y	N	N	Y	Y	P
A	A	A	R	A	M	F	O	R	T	H	L
P	R	I	M	M	E	D	E	A	L	L	Y
K	A	R	E	S	I	D	E	N	T	S	N
F	T	P	T	A	F	T	P	A	I	R	X

In the puzzle above, find the homonyms for . . .

pail	plane	rights
ferry	hole	fourth
sum	hare	steel
week	fare	route
aloud	pear, pare	stairs
tail	residence	pane
links	carrot	

This Day in September

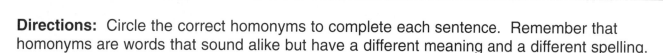

Directions: Circle the correct homonyms to complete each sentence. Remember that homonyms are words that sound alike but have a different meaning and a different spelling.

September 1

The United States entered World War II on September 1, 1939. This (**wore, war**) came to be the deadliest war ever, because more people (**died, dyed**) in it than any other war in history.

September 4

On this date in 1880, George Eastman created the first camera that used (**roles, rolls**) of film. (**Eight, Ate**) years later, he invented the first portable camera.

September 11

Henry Hudson was the first person to explore the Hudson River. He began his exploration on this date in 1609. The Hudson River has since become an important commercial waterway, because the (**Erie, Eerie**) Canal (**links, lynx**) it to the Great Lakes and the Atlantic Ocean.

September 16

The Mayflower left Plymouth, England, on this date in 1620. (**Their, There**) were 102 Pilgrims aboard, heading to America. When they arrived, they named (**their, there**) new home Plymouth Rock.

September 18

The United States Air Force became a separate military service on this date in 1947. Before this time, it was a branch of the United States Army. Currently, the (**principal, principle**) difference between the (**to, too, two**) is that the Air Force protects the air and the Army protects the land.

September 20

On this date in 1859, George Simpson received a patent (**fore, for**) the electric stove.

September 24

The United States Supreme Court was created on this date in 1789. (**It's, Its**) the highest (**court, quart**) in the United States. (**They're, There**) are nine justices of the Supreme Court. They (**meat, meet**) in Washington, D.C.

September Crossword

Find the homonyms for . . .

Across

3. threw
4. vain/vein
5. pear/pare
6. pear/pair
9. fined
10. nun
12. wok
13. stairs
15. carrot
16. brake
17. weak

Down

1. steel
2. principal
4. vane/vain
5. pane
7. role
8. links
11. stake
12. rap
14. seen

September Word Search

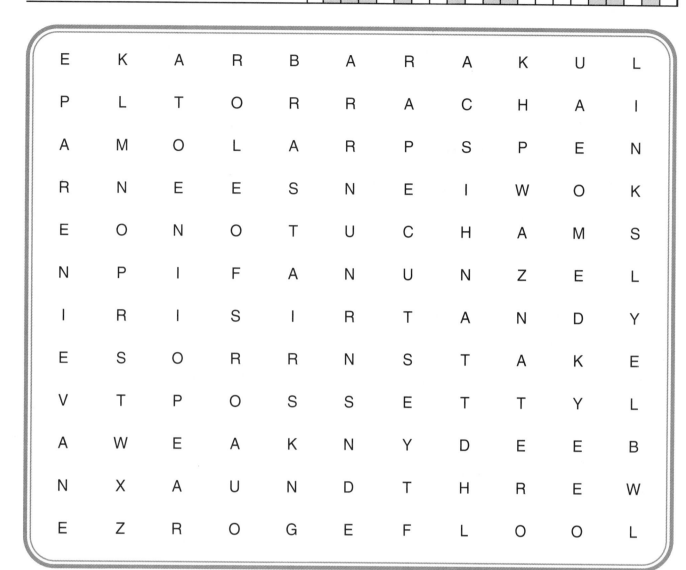

```
E   K   A   R   B   A   R   A   K   U   L
P   L   T   O   R   R   A   C   H   A   I
A   M   O   L   A   R   P   S   P   E   N
R   N   E   E   S   N   E   I   W   O   K
E   O   N   O   T   U   C   H   A   M   S
N   P   I   F   A   N   U   N   Z   E   L
I   R   I   S   I   R   T   A   N   D   Y
E   S   O   R   R   N   S   T   A   K   E
V   T   P   O   S   S   E   T   T   Y   L
A   W   E   A   K   N   Y   D   E   E   B
N   X   A   U   N   D   T   H   R   E   W
E   Z   R   O   G   E   F   L   O   O   L
```

In the puzzle above, find the homonyms for . . .

none	roll	wrap
principle	through	steak
vein, vain	pain	vane, vain
break	carat	pair, pear
lynx	pare, pair	find
week	stares	scene
steal	walk	

This Day in October

Directions: Circle the correct homonyms to complete each sentence. Remember that homonyms are words that sound alike but have a different meaning and a different spelling.

October 2

Jules Verne was an author and pioneer in science fiction. He used science principles and his imagination in his (**writing, righting**). He anticipated the airplane, submarine, television, and space travel in his fiction writing. On this date in 1873, he introduced his book entitled *Around the World in Eighty* (***Days, Daze***).

October 7

On this date in 1986, U.S. President Ronald W. Reagan signed a bill that (**maid, made**) the rose the national (**flour, flower**). Roses are beautiful, elegant, and fragrant.

October 9

The Fingerprint Society was founded on October 9, 1915. Fingerprints are used as a method of identification because the underside tips of the fingers and thumbs (**have, halve**) ridges that are unique (**to, too, two**) each person.

October 15

The Statue of Liberty was designated a national monument on this date in 1924. The statue was a gift from the people of France to the people of the United States; it has stood in the (**Knew, New**) York Harbor since it first arrived in 1885.

October 16

Today is Dictionary Day. Noah Webster, author of the first American dictionary, was born on this date in 1758. He wrote the first American dictionary; it took more than twenty years to complete. Although Webster died in 1843, many modern dictionaries still (**bare, bear**) his name.

October 21

Alfred Nobel was born on October 21, 1833. His estate has provided funds (**four, for**) the annual Nobel Prize since 1901. These prizes are awarded to those recognized for their work in such fields as (**peace, piece**), literature, and medicine.

October 29

The U.S. (**stalk, stock**) market crashed on October 29, 1929. This day, known as Black Tuesday, signaled the beginning of the (**Great, Grate**) Depression.

October Crossword

Find the homonyms for . . .

Across

3. chute
4. paws
6. grown
7. effect
10. rain/rein
11. straight
12. find
13. beau
14. scene
15. sweet

Down

1. navel
2. yoke
3. shear
5. days
6. gait
8. claws
9. nose
11. shown
12. flour
13. berth

October Word Search

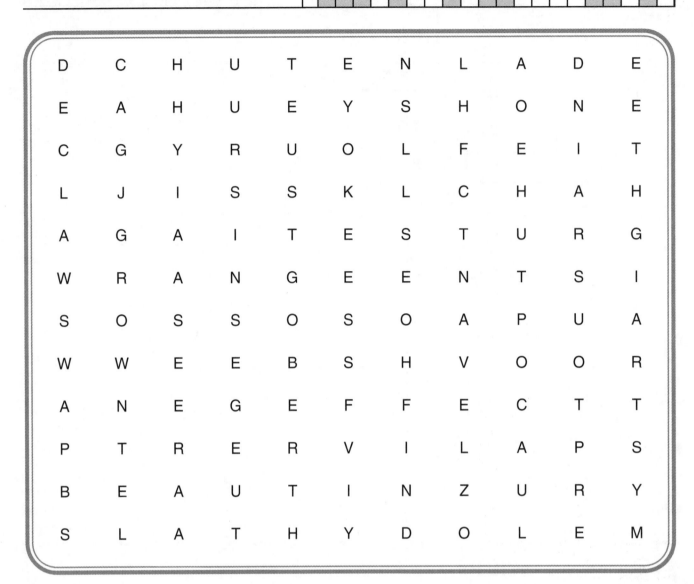

D	C	H	U	T	E	N	L	A	D	E
E	A	H	U	E	Y	S	H	O	N	E
C	G	Y	R	U	O	L	F	E	I	T
L	J	I	S	S	K	L	C	H	A	H
A	G	A	I	T	E	S	T	U	R	G
W	R	A	N	G	E	E	N	T	S	I
S	O	S	S	O	S	O	A	P	U	A
W	W	E	E	B	S	H	V	O	O	R
A	N	E	G	E	F	F	E	C	T	T
P	T	R	E	R	V	I	L	A	P	S
B	E	A	U	T	I	N	Z	U	R	Y
S	L	A	T	H	Y	D	O	L	E	M

In the puzzle above, find the homonyms for . . .

fined	suite	bow
seen	reign, rein	shown
affect	shoot	yolk
flower	pause	sheer
birth	clause	gate
daze	knows	strait
naval	groan	

This Day in November

Directions: Circle the correct homonyms to complete each sentence. Remember that homonyms are words that sound alike but have a different meaning and a different spelling.

November 3

John Montague, Earl of Sandwich, was born November 3, 1718. He was the first person to put (**meat, meet**) between (**too, two**) slices of bread and make a sandwich. Do you like your sandwich with mayonnaise or (**mustered, mustard**)?

November 5

On this date in 1935, Parker Brothers introduced Monopoly. It's the best selling (**board, bored**) game in history.

November 15

Zebulon Pike discovered Pike's (**Peak, Peek**) in Colorado on this date in 1806. (**It's, Its**) 14,110 (**feat, feet**) at (**it's, its**) highest point.

November 17

The Suez Canal opened on this date in 1869. The canal is about 100 miles long and cuts over 4,000 miles off the (**route, root**) between Britain and India.

November 21

Baseball player Ken Griffey, Jr., was born on 11-21-69. He and his father, Ken Griffey, Sr., were the first father and (**son, sun**) (**pear, pair**) to hit home runs for the same (**team, teem**) in the same game in major league baseball history.

November 25

Andrew Carnegie was born on November 25, 1835. He believed that the duty of the rich is to distribute their surplus wealth to the (**pour, poor**) and to those in (**need, kneed, knead**). He set up many charitable foundations and educational institutions.

November 30

Mark Twain was born on this date in 1835. (**Some, Sum**) authors use a name other than the name they were born with when they (**write, right**). Twain is one of these authors: his (**reel, real**) name is Samuel Clements.

November Crossword

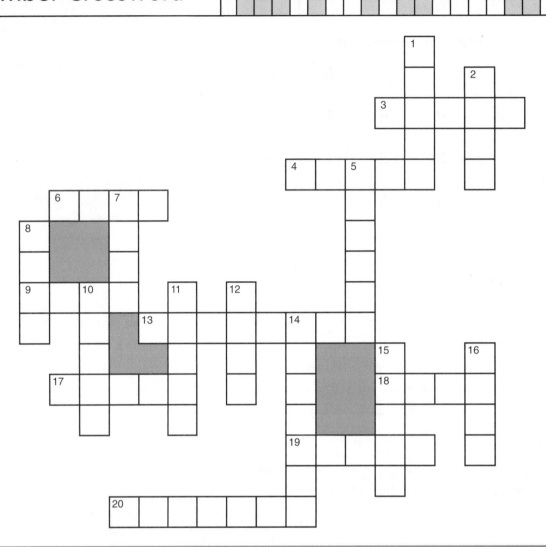

Find the homonyms for . . .

Across

3. board
4. sheer
6. mined
9. yolk
13. strait
17. navel
18. lain
19. shone
20. mustered

Down

1. flower
2. team
5. affect
7. knows
8. daze
10. need/kneed
11. stock
12. gate
14. guest
15. clause
16. bow

November Word Search

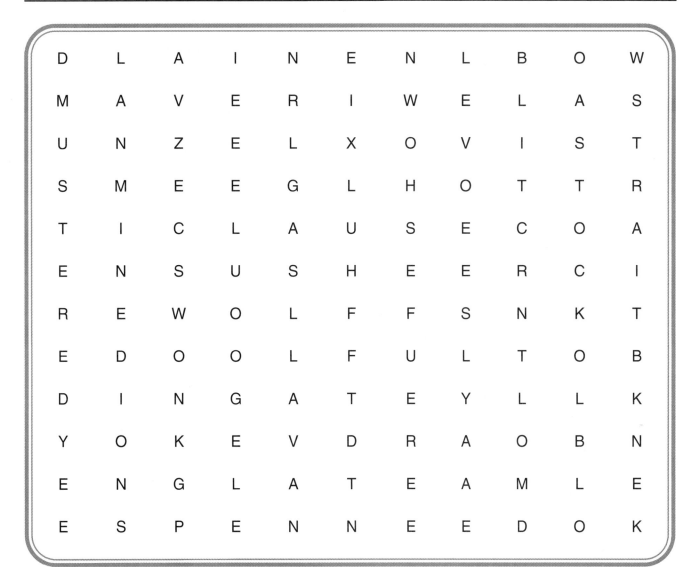

```
D   L   A   I   N   E   N   L   B   O   W
M   A   V   E   R   I   W   E   L   A   S
U   N   Z   E   L   X   O   V   I   S   T
S   M   E   E   G   L   H   O   T   T   R
T   I   C   L   A   U   S   E   C   O   A
E   N   S   U   S   H   E   E   R   C   I
R   E   W   O   L   F   F   S   N   K   T
E   D   O   O   L   F   U   L   T   O   B
D   I   N   G   A   T   E   Y   L   L   K
Y   O   K   E   V   D   R   A   O   B   N
E   N   G   L   A   T   E   A   M   L   E
E   S   P   E   N   N   E   E   D   O   K
```

In the puzzle above, find the homonyms for . . .

effect	beau	mustard
flour	shone	teem
days	yoke	bored
navel	shear	knead/kneed
claws	gait	lane
nose	straight	mind
stalk	guessed	

This Day in December

Directions: Circle the correct homonyms to complete each sentence. Remember that homonyms are words that sound alike but have a different meaning and a different spelling.

December 1

On December 1, 1955, Rosa Parks was arrested in Montgomery, Alabama, for refusing to give up her bus seat to a white passenger. This was the beginning of the civil (**writes, rights**) movement.

December 6

On December 6, 1933, a ban was lifted on James Joyce's novel *Ulysses*. (**Dew, Do, Due**) you know that when a book or any other work of art is (**band, banned**) (**dew, do, due**) to its content, that's called censorship?

December 7

On the (**mourning, morning**) of December 7, 1941, the Japanese attacked Pearl Harbor, Hawaii. This event (**lead, led**) to the official beginning of the United States' involvement in World War II.

December 8

The first greeting card was printed on this date in 1843. John C. Horsley designed both the (**versus, verses**) and illustrations.

December 15

The first ten amendments were added to the U.S. Constitution on this date in 1791. These are also known as the Bill of Rights because they define and protect the rights of the people. Since then, several additional amendments have (**been, bin**) added. These amendments have (**aloud, allowed**) for change and growth to (**meat, meet**) the needs of the American people.

December 17

Today is Wright Brothers' Day. We celebrate the first successful airplane flight that took place on this date in 1903, at Kitty Hawk, North Carolina. The (**plane, plain**) flight was a (**vary, very**) short one, but it marked the beginning of a new era in (**air, heir**) travel.

December 31

Baseball (**great, grate**) Roberto Clemente died on December 31, 1972, (**wile, while**) flying supplies to earthquake victims in Nicaragua.

December Crossword

Find the homonyms for . . .

Across

3. mind
6. flu
8. passed
10. guessed
12. mustard
13. wait
15. sites/cites
17. peak/pique
18. board
19. do/due

Down

1. lane
2. peal
4. cent/scent
5. shoot
7. waist
9. cents
11. size
13. walk
14. kneed/knead
16. heard

December Word Search

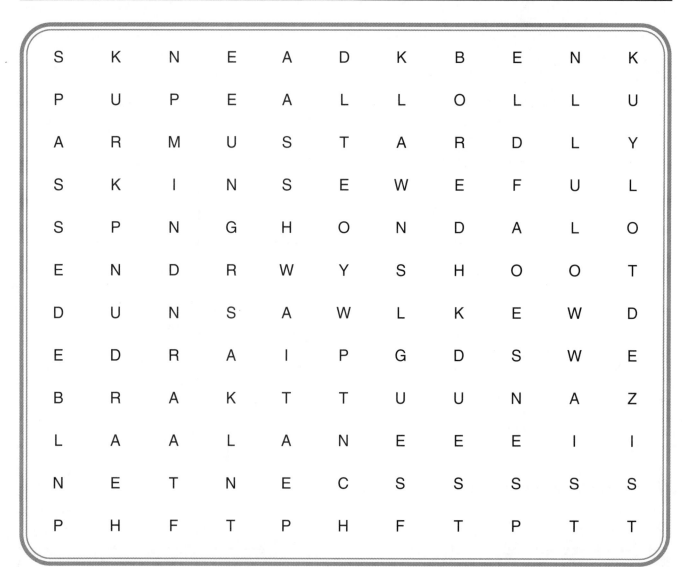

```
S   K   N   E   A   D   K   B   E   N   K
P   U   P   E   A   L   L   O   L   L   U
A   R   M   U   S   T   A   R   D   L   Y
S   K   I   N   S   E   W   E   F   U   L
S   P   N   G   H   O   N   D   A   L   O
E   N   D   R   W   Y   S   H   O   O   T
D   U   N   S   A   W   L   K   E   W   D
E   D   R   A   I   P   G   D   S   W   E
B   R   A   K   T   T   U   U   N   A   Z
L   A   A   L   A   N   E   E   E   I   I
N   E   T   N   E   C   S   S   S   S   S
P   H   F   T   P   H   F   T   P   T   T
```

In the puzzle above, find the homonyms for . . .

guessed	lain	flew
mustered	waste	peel
board	weight	sent/cent
need/kneed	mined	past
scents/cents	sighs	chute
peek	wok	herd
sights, cites	dew/do	

Holidas of the Year

January 15

Martin Luther King, Jr., was born in Atlanta, Georgia, on this date in 1929. This day is celebrated as a national holiday on the third Monday of January. He was a leader in civil rights; he believed in nonviolent protests, (**not, knot**) violent one. Do you (**know, no**) that civil rights are the rights and privileges of citizens to nondiscriminatory treatment and a (**bettor, better**) way of life?

February 14

Today is Valentine's Day. Pink and (**red, read**) are the colors of the day. Chocolates and (**flours, flowers**) are the gifts to give. Love is in the (**heir, air**).

March 17

Today is St. Patrick's Day, an ethnic (**or, oar, ore**) regional holiday. (**Its, It's**) celebrated as the anniversary of the death of Patrick, Ireland's patron saint. Shamrock leaves, green clothing, and pots of gold all make this day a fun celebration.

April 1

(**Be, Bee**) extra aware today! It's April Fool's Day, which means that someone could try to play a trick on (**you, ewe**).

October 31

Halloween is celebrated on this day. It's a (**grate, great**) time, especially for those who have a (**sweet, suite**) tooth. In addition to the candy treats, we see lots of ghosts, goblins, bats, and maybe even a (**witch, which**) or two.

November 27

Thanksgiving Day is celebrated on the last Thursday in November. This tradition started in 1621, a year after the pilgrims landed in the (**new, knew**) (**whirled, world**).

December 24

Christmas Eve is celebrated by many on this day. The custom of Santa Claus bringing (**presence, presents**) on the night before Christmas started long ago when the Dutch first came to America. Since Santa is (**so, sew**) busy, he does not have time to (**rap, wrap**) the gifts. Instead, he just leaves them under the tree.

Holidays Crossword

Find the homonyms for . . .

Across

4. bred
7. days
8. mall
9. cell
12. weighs
13. bread
15. pray
17. steak
18. vain/vein

Down

1. hare
2. paced
3. find
4. bawl
5. praise
6. break
9. soar
10. laze
11. lays
14. read
16. faun

Holidays Word Search

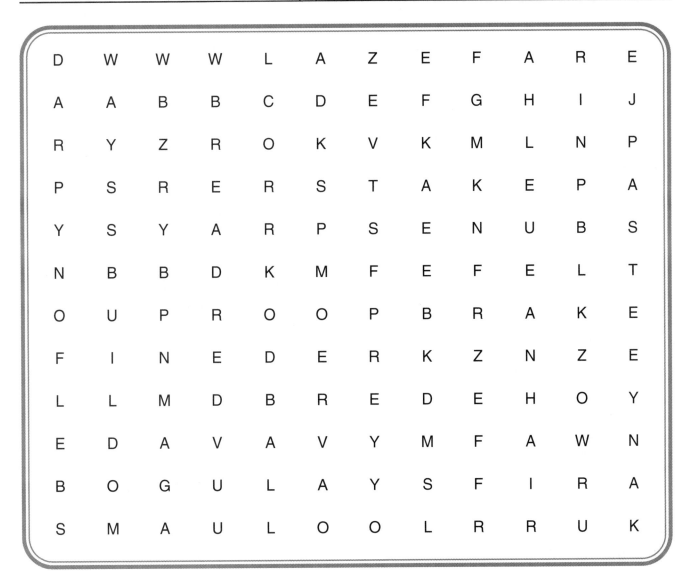

D	W	W	W	L	A	Z	E	F	A	R	E
A	A	B	B	C	D	E	F	G	H	I	J
R	Y	Z	R	O	K	V	K	M	L	N	P
P	S	R	E	R	S	T	A	K	E	P	A
Y	S	Y	A	R	P	S	E	N	U	B	S
N	B	B	D	K	M	F	E	F	E	L	T
O	U	P	R	O	O	P	B	R	A	K	E
F	I	N	E	D	E	R	K	Z	N	Z	E
L	L	M	D	B	R	E	D	E	H	O	Y
E	D	A	V	A	V	Y	M	F	A	W	N
B	O	G	U	L	A	Y	S	F	I	R	A
S	M	A	U	L	O	O	L	R	R	U	K

In the puzzle above, find the homonyms for . . .

days	faun	bread
weighs	bawl	lays
paced	fair	laze
mall	hare	pray
vein/vain	steak	praise/preys
read	break	billed
find	bred	

Answer Key

Page 3

January 1: New, pause, ring, new

January 5: died, to

January 8: roll, Blue

January 17: weather, rough, flew

January 22: rain, hail, mail

January 25: heard

January 31: born, great, him

Page 4

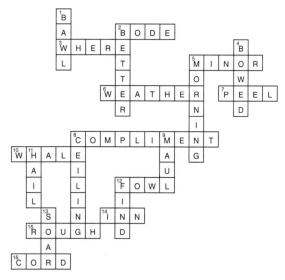

Page 5

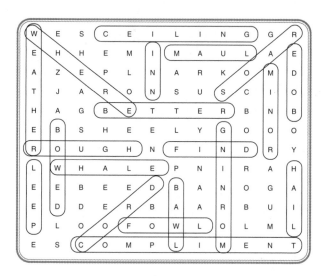

Page 6

February 2: have, not, see

February 7: wrote, praise

February 11: instance

February 19: our, sun

February 23: all, by

February 26: in, wear

February 29: sun, which, it's

Page 7

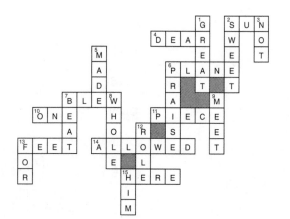

Page 8

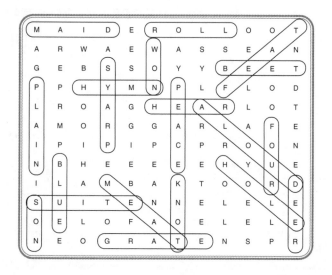

Answer Key

Page 9

March 2: you'll, your

March 7: sell, right

March 19: forward, passed, hour

March 21: It's, sun, night

March 23: or, peace, vain

March 28: for, in

March 31: Have, been, Would

Page 10

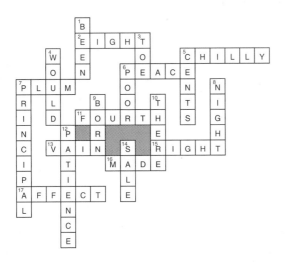

Page 11

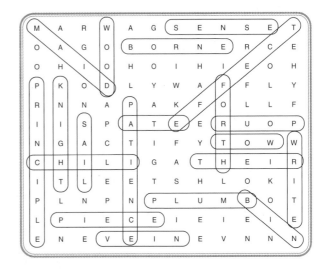

Page 12

April 2: fairy, tales

April 5: effect, patients, very

April 6: fourth, all

April 14: died, sea

April 15: in, there

April 18: rode, to, to

April 26: which, size

April 29: time, sell

Page 13

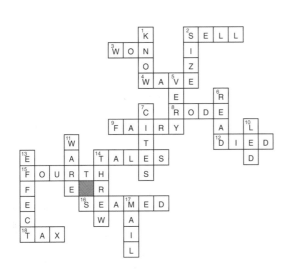

Page 14

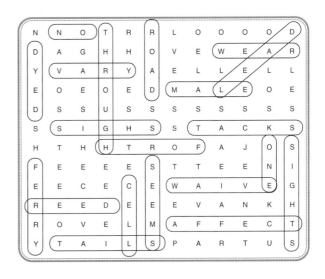

Answer Key

Page 15

May 2: all, for, canvas

May 6: for, break

May 10: to

May 14: in, ought, know

May 17: made, in

May 24: mode, two

May 28: one, muscle

Page 16

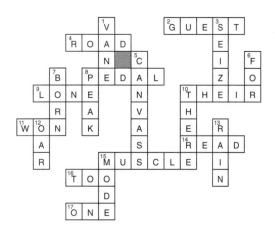

Page 17

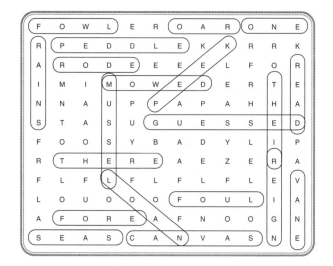

Page 18

June 2: great, died, it's

June 6: beach, led

June 8: in, pie, be

June 13: have, right, or

June 16: beat, one, made

June 21: rays, there, hours

June 27: hear, see, read

Page 19

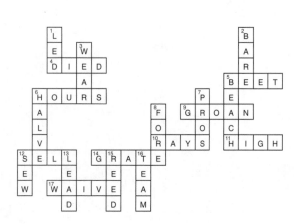

Page 20

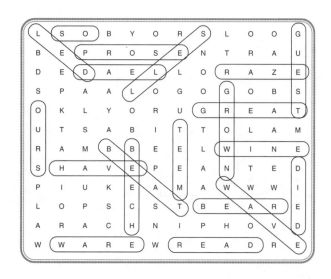

Answer Key

Page 21

July 5: great, him, tide

July 10: site, capital

July 13: You'll, know

July 15: all, night

July 16: Pole, in

July 20: to, feet, one, one, eight

July 24: made, by

Page 22

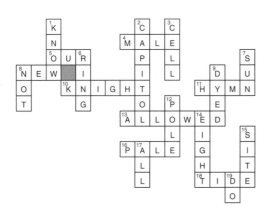

Page 23

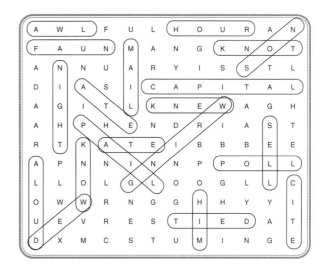

Page 24

August 3: made, It's

August 4: tax, tax

August 8: heart, for

August 12: Some, by

August 22: War, or

August 24: residence

August 30: whole, week

Page 25

Page 26

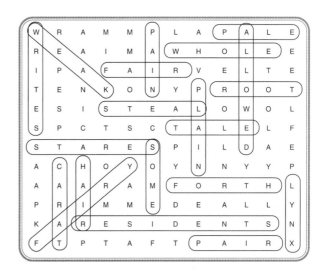

Answer Key

Page 27

September 1: war, died

September 4: rolls, Eight

September 11: Erie, links

September 16: There, their

September 18: principle, two

September 20: for

September 24: It's, court, There, meet

Page 28

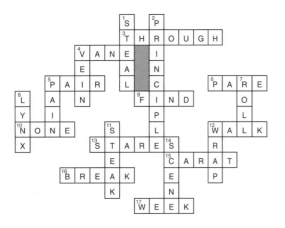

Page 29

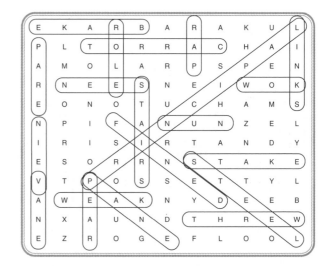

Page 30

October 2: writing, Days

October 7: made, flower

October 9: have, to

October 15: New

October 16: bear

October 21: for, peace

October 29: stock, Great

Page 31

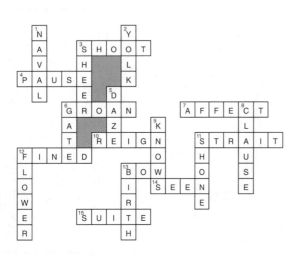

Page 32

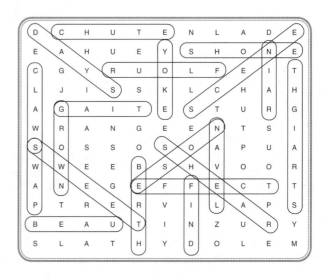

Answer Key

Page 33

November 3: meat, two, mustard

November 5: board

November 15: Peak, It's, feet, its

November 17: route

November 21: son, pair, team

November 25: poor, need

November 30: Some, write, real

Page 34

Page 35

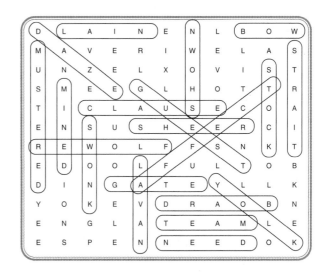

Page 36

December 1: rights

December 6: Do, banned, due

December 7: morning, led

December 8: verses

December 15: been, allowed, meet

December 17: plane, very, air

December 31: great, while

Page 37

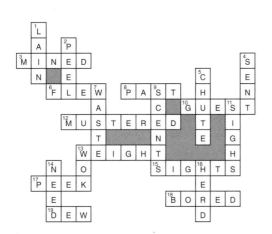

Page 38

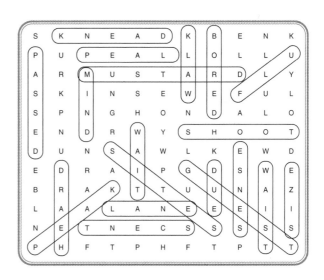

Answer Key

Page 39

January 15: know, better

February 14: red, flowers, air

March 17: or, It's

April 1: Be, you

October 31: great, sweet, witch

November 27: new, world

December 24: presents, so, wrap

Page 40

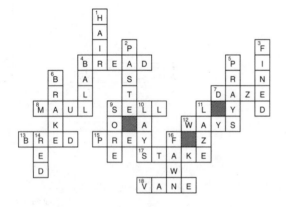

Page 41

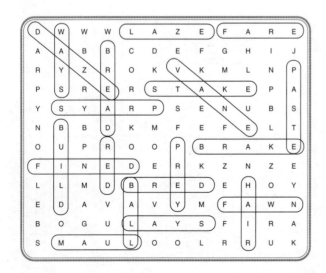